A Tribute to
THE YOUNG AT HEART

MAURICE SENDAK

By Julie Berg

Published by Abdo & Daughters, 4940 Viking Drive Suite 622, Edina, Minnesota 55435.

Library bound edition distributed by Rockbottom Books, Pentagon Tower, P.O. Box 36036, Minneapolis, Minnesota 55435.

Cover photo -   Black Star

Photo credits - Wide World, pgs. 5, 10, 14, 16, 22, 28

Edited by Rosemary Wallner

LIBRARY OF CONGRESS CATALOGING-IN-PUBLICATION DATA
Berg, Julie,
    Maurice Sendak / written by Julie Berg.
        p. cm. -- (Young at Heart)
    Includes Glossary.
    Summary: Presents the life of the artist known primarily for his award-winning illustrated children's books.
    ISBN 1-56239-225-5
    1. Sendak, Maurice--Juvenile literature. 2. Illustrators--United States--Biography--Juvenile literature. [1. Sendak, Maurice. 2. Illustrators.] I. Title. II. Series.
    NC975.5.S44B47   1993
    741.6'42'092--dc20
    [B]   93-15738
                                                              CIP
                                                              AC

TABLE OF CONTENTS

A RESPECTED ILLUSTRATOR

Maurice Sendak is an unusual success story. As a child, he was sick much of the time. He hated school, and did not make friends easily. But he enjoyed drawing. Over the years, he taught himself to draw by imitating some of the best book artists in the world.

Eventually, Sendak became one of the world's most respected illustrators. His controversial book, *Where the Wild Things Are,* won him international acclaim. It also won the Caldecott Medal, the highest award for children's books.

According to Sendak, the qualities that make for excellence in children's literature can be summed up in a single word: imagination. That's the main ingredient in all his books.

Maurice Sendak became one of the world's most
well-known illustrators. *Where the Wild Things Are*
won him international acclaim.

A SICKLY CHILDHOOD

Maurice Sendak was born June 10, 1928, in Brooklyn, New York. Sendak was the youngest of three children. His parents, Philip and Sarah Sendak, came to America from Poland before World War I. Some of Sendak's happiest times were spent with his father, who introduced him to the art of storytelling.

"During my childhood, which seemed like one long series of illnesses," Sendak said, "he invented beautiful imaginative tales to tell me and my brother and sister. He was a marvelous improvisor and would often extend a story for several nights."

When Sendak was two years old, he contracted measles. Soon after, he became inflicted with pneumonia. The disease left him frail and delicate. It also made him fearful of dying.

"I think a lot of children are scared of dying," he recalled. "But I was scared because I heard talk of [death] all around me. There was always the possibility I might have died of the measles or its aftermath. Certainly my parents were afraid I wouldn't survive."

Once, when he was older, he asked for a sled. His father replied, "You, a sled? You'll have pneumonia in a week."

Young Sendak was miserable. He couldn't make friends. He couldn't play stoopball or skate. Instead, he stayed home and drew pictures. Because of this, his friends called him a "sissy."

"When I wanted to go out and do something," Sendak recalled, "my father would say, 'You'll catch cold.' And I did. I did whatever he told me."

Even at a young age, Sendak knew he was an observer, not a doer. He often watched his grandmother and dreamed up different stories about her. Sendak was so aware of the streets on which he lived, he could describe them in complete detail—how many houses there were, who lived in which one, and what the neighbors looked like.

THE FIRST BOOK

In 1934, Sendak produced his first book with his eleven-year-old brother, Jack. The book was called *They Were Inseparable.* "It was a naive and funny book," Sendak said. "We both idolized our sister. She was the eldest and by far the prettiest child, and we thought she was the crown jewel of the family."

Because they adored her, Sendak and his brother made the book about a brother and a sister. At the very end of the story, there is an accident. The brother is in the hospital, and they don't think he is going to recover. Suddenly, the sister comes rushing in, and the two of them embrace as they cry, "We are inseparable!" Everyone tries to pull them apart, but they jump out the hospital window together.

Sendak hated school from the first grade on. He still feels that formal education saps imagination and free, creative play. "I hate, loathe, and despise schools," he said. "The only part of my childhood that was truly punishing and suffering was school. Perhaps it's a rationalization, because I hated it so much. But school is bad for you if you have any talent.

You should be cultivating that talent in your own particular way."

In order to go to school each day, Sendak had to talk himself into it. He could not stand being in crowded classrooms. And he never liked to compete. He was often so embarrassed and unsure of himself that he stammered.

MARK TWAIN AND MICKEY MOUSE

In the 1930s, Sendak didn't own any "official" children's books he considered "classics." The only books he had were cheap paperbacks and comic books. In 1937, Sendak received his first "real" book from his sister on his ninth birthday. It was *The Prince and the Pauper* by Mark Twain.

Sendak developed a ritual with the book. He set it up on a table and stared at it for a long time. It wasn't because he was so impressed with Mark Twain. Rather, he considered the book a beautiful object.

Mickey Mouse was Sendak's favorite childhood character.
The above photo shows Walt Disney illustrating his
most famous character.

After he stared at the book, Sendak would smell it. The book was printed on fine paper and had a shiny cover. And it was solid and bound tightly. Then came another strange ritual.

"I remember trying to bite into it," he said, "which I didn't imagine is what my sister intended when she bought the book for me. But the last thing I did with the book was to read it. It was all right. But I think it started then, a passion for books and bookmaking."

Sendak wanted to be an illustrator very early in his life. There was so much more to a book than just reading it. For many books, there were also illustrations to enjoy. Mickey Mouse and the Disney books were early childhood favorites. "I remember a Mickey Mouse mask that came on a big box of cornflakes," he said. "What a fantastic mask! Such a big, bright, vivid, gorgeous hunk of face! And that's what a kid in Brooklyn knew at the time."

Mickey Mouse was Sendak's "common street friend." He chewed Mickey Mouse gum. He brushed his teeth with a Mickey Mouse toothbrush. And he played with Mickey Mouse in a variety of games. "Best of all," recalled Sendak, "our street pal was also a movie star.

In the darkened theater, the sudden flash of his brilliant, wild, joyful face, radiating great golden beams, filled me with pleasure."

But in school, Sendak learned to despise Walt Disney. Sendak was told that Disney corrupted the fairy tale and was in poor taste. This caused Sendak to review his fondness for Mickey Mouse.

"It took me nearly twenty years to rediscover the pleasure of that first, truthful response and to fuse it with my own work as an artist," Sendak said. "It took me just as long to forget the corrupting effect of school."

LEARNING TO DRAW

Between 1941 and 1945, Sendak attended Lafayette High School in New York. There, he began his career as an illustrator for All-American Comics. Sendak filled in the backgrounds for the "Mutt and Jeff" comic strip.

Because he hated school, Sendak felt more comfortable learning by himself.

Many of the artists who influenced him were illustrators he accidentally came upon. He knew that George Cruikshank illustrated *Grimm's Fairy Tales.* So he looked at everything Cruikshank illustrated and copied his style. He wanted to crosshatch the way Cruikshank did.

Then Sendak discovered Wilhelm Busch and found all his books. Much to Sendak's delight, he discovered that Busch also crosshatched. Sendak studied these two illustrators, and his talent grew.

In 1947, Sendak's first book was published. It was called *Atomics for the Millions.* One of Sendak's high school teachers wrote the book. Sendak drew all of the illustrations.

In 1948, Sendak built animated wooden toys with his brother. They brought the toys to F.A.O. Schwarz, a famous toy store in New York City. Executives admired the toys, but they felt that the figures would be too expensive to mass produce. Still, the company hired Sendak as a window-display director. He worked at the store for three years. In the evening, he attended classes at the Art Students League.

F.A.O. Schwarz is a famous toy store in New York where Sendak worked
as a window-display director while attending art school.

GETTING PUBLISHED

Sendak's big break in book publishing came in 1950. He was introduced to Ursula Nordstrom. She was a children's book editor at Harper and Brothers. Nordstrom offered Sendak his first chance to illustrate a children's book. It was called *The Wonderful Farm* by Marcel Ayme.

"I loved her on the first meeting," Sendak said of Nordstrom. "My happiest memories, in fact, are of my earliest career, when Ursula was my confidante and best friend. She really became my home and the person I trusted most. Those beginning years revolved around my trips to the old Harper offices on Thirty-third Street and being fed books by Ursula, as well as encouraged with every drawing I did.

"We had our disagreements," he continued. "But she treated me like a hothouse flower, watered me for ten years, and handpicked the works that were to become my permanent backlist and bread-and-butter support. Ursula is not only an enormously gifted editor. She's generous of herself with young people and makes an incredible personal investment in their careers."

Sendak worked with many talented authors. Here he is signing
a print from his *Mother Goose Collection*.

In 1952, Sendak illustrated Ruth Krauss' *A Hole Is to Dig.* He spent his weekends in Connecticut with the author and her husband. Krauss was an experienced children's book author and a patient teacher. Sendak claimed that 80 percent of the book's layout ideas came from Krauss. Still, the book established Sendak's reputation as a major children's book illustrator.

The following year, Sendak traveled to Europe. There he gained more experience illustrating Ayme's *The Magic Pictures.*

The book gave Sendak the perfect chance to show his feelings for southern France. He did not want to make direct replicas of the wonderful little towns. Instead, he wanted to show the charming qualities of the book's two little girls, Delphine and Marinette. He also wanted them to stand for all that France meant to him.

In 1956, Sendak wrote his first book, *Very Far Away.* He had greater confidence in himself as an author. Fantasy was an important part of the book.

"I don't think there's any part of our lives, as adults or children, when we're not fantasizing," said Sendak. "But we prefer to relegate that activity to children, as if fantasy were some tomfoolery only for immature minds. Children do live in both fantasy and reality. They move back and forth with ease, in a way that we no longer remember how to do. Fantasy is the core of all writing for children, as I think it is for the writing of any book. Certainly it is crucial to my work. There is probably no such thing as creativity without fantasy."

ROSIE

In 1960, Sendak created one of his favorite characters in the book, *The Sign on Rosie's Door.* Rosie was a fierce child who impressed Sendak with her ability to imagine herself into being anything she wanted to be, anywhere in or out of the world. Her tremendous energy activated Sendak's own creativity. The first sketches of Rosie were made from the window of his parents' apartment in 1948 and 1949.

"My earliest reference to her appears in a tattered, homemade sketchbook titled 'Brooklyn Kids, August 1948,' " said Sendak. "I was twenty and she was ten. We never officially met. Once, however, when we passed on the street, she saluted me with a 'Hi, Johnson!' Bewildering, but typically Rosie. I don't recall her taking any further notice of me. Though she must have been aware of the pasty-faced youth (me) watching from a second-floor window."

At the time, Sendak was out of work and out of money. He lived at home and did not know what to do next. Rosie preoccupied him. She made him forget his misery. He filled his notebooks with ideas that later found their way into every one of his children's books.

"My *Nutshell Library* is tied to *The Sign on Rosie's Door,*" Sendak said. "Alligator, Pierre, Johnny and the nameless hero of *Chicken Soup with Rice* are modeled on the 'men' in Rosie's life."

THE WILD THINGS

By 1962, Sendak was thirty-four years old. He had illustrated fifty books, seven of which he had written. In 1963, Sendak created one of his most popular and controversial books, *Where the Wild Things Are.* It was a fantasy, originally written in 1955 in an unpublished work, *Where the Wild Horses Are.*

Sendak, however, could not draw horses. So he had to find something else to draw instead. For the longest time, he did not know what to use as a substitute. He tried many different animals in the title, but they just did not sound right.

"Finally, I lit on 'things,'" recalled Sendak. "But what would 'things' look like? I wanted my wild things to be frightening. But why? It was probably at this point that I remembered how I detested my Brooklyn relatives as a small child. They came almost every Sunday, and there was my week-long anxiety about their coming next Sunday. My mother always cooked for them. And as I saw it, they were eating up all our food."

Sendak had to wear good clothes for these aunts, uncles, and cousins. Ugly plastic covers were put over the furniture. Sendak's relatives were not good at making small talk with children.

"There you'd be," he said, "sitting on a kitchen chair, totally, helpless, while they cooed over you and pinched your cheeks. Or they'd lean way over with their bad teeth and hairy noses, and say something like, 'You're so cute, I could eat you up.' And I knew if my mother didn't hurry up with the cooking, they probably would."

Many librarians felt the book was too scary for small children. Despite some negative book reviews, *Where the Wild Things Are* became a tremendous success. It has been published in thirteen foreign languages.

"With *Where the Wild Things Are,*" Sendak said at the time, "I feel that I am at the end of a long apprenticeship. By that I mean all my previous work now seems to have been an elaborate preparation for it. I believe it is an immense step forward for me, a critical stage in my work."

Sendak stands next to one of his most famous characters.
For his book *Where the Wild Things Are*, Sendak won the
Caldecott Medal, the highest honor for a children's book illustrator.

The following year, Sendak won the Caldecott Medal for *Where the Wild Things Are.* It is the highest award for a children's book.

THE HEART ATTACK

Sendak was on top of the children's book world. His future never seemed brighter. But then, in May 1967, he suffered a major heart attack during a trip to England.

"I was amazed," he recalled. "I couldn't believe it was happening, that my mission could be cut short like that. I felt as though a bargain had been broken, that so long as I kept working and honestly recalling my childhood, I had been granted some sort of immunity."

But Sendak was not immune to health problems, and he returned home. That's when he discovered that his favorite dog, Jennie, had cancer. It was all a nightmare, but Sendak had to do something difficult. He asked a friend to take the dog to the veterinarian where it was put to sleep.

Less than one month after Jennie's death, *Higglety, Piglety, Pop!: or There Must Be More to Life* was published. The book was a tribute to his dog.

"I wrote it when Jennie was getting old," recalled Sendak, "and I was afraid she was going to die. Somehow it was easier to work up an anxiety about the dog's dying than about my mother [who died of cancer in 1968], because that was just too much to go for."

MORE BOOKS

In 1970, Sendak produced *In the Night Kitchen,* one of his most memorable picture books. It was based on an advertisement for the Sunshine Bakers that Sendak saw as a child. The advertisement read "We Bake While You Sleep." Sendak decided to show exactly how it happened.

In the Night Kitchen took two years of concentrated work. Sendak found the experience fulfilling, and shed some light on his creative process.

"During that time," he said, "you are completely absorbed in this dream, this fantasy. The pleasure you get is extraordinary. You live in a very strange world, really quite divorced from this dull, real world. When I'm working on a book, I see very few people, do very few things but think about my book, dream about my book, love it, hate it, pull hairs out of my head. And the only time I speak to people is when I want to complain about it. And then it's over, and then it's finished, and the great shock comes when it's printed.

"A book being printed is a major topic in itself," he added. "It is a very difficult thing to see through. What was once very dreamlike and transparent and what you thought was a magic moment has now become a real thing in a printing press. And it's going through a big machine, and it looks lousy, and it has to be done all over again. And so gradually your particular transparent little dream is becoming more real, and more terrible every moment. And then finally it is a book. And you become extremely depressed, because you realize that what was so superb and different is really just another book! How strange. It is a totally different experience. It takes me a long time to shift gears."

In 1971, Sendak shifted gears to concentrate on a collection of Grimm fairy tales. The collection was to be called *The Juniper Tree*. He made the trip to Germany to research the regions where the Grimm brothers had collected their tales.

Returning to New York, Sendak bought an apartment on Fifth Avenue and a house in Ridgefield, Connecticut. He also bought a golden retriever named Io and a German shepard named Erda. When Erda had puppies, Sendak kept one and named him Agamemnon.

THE ANIMATED FILM

In 1975, Sendak wrote and produced a half-hour animated film. He called it "Really Rosie Starring the Nutshell Kids." It aired on CBS-TV on February 19. Sendak had remembered the Disney cartoons of his childhood. He had wanted to make an animated film of his own.

Sheldon Riss, a producer, approached him with the idea. At first, Sendak was hesitant. "In the world of book publishing," he said, "I have command over my work; how it is printed and presented.

I feared losing it in the world of networks, among the vast crew of collaborators necessary for such a project. I held out for two years. Happily, so did Riss. There was no clink of coin in his enthusiasm, and his excitement and optimism finally won me over."

Once he had committed himself to the animated film, Sendak decided to play it safe and stick to what he knew best: his fantasy-plagued Brooklyn kids. The show was about the ability of the kids to overcome the boredom of a long summer's day on an ordinary street.

"We vowed to pay attention to detail," Sendak said. "We concentrated on content, and we let the form of the show evolve naturally. . .as naturally, I hoped, as children playing in the street."

In 1976, Sendak illustrated Randall Jarrell's last book for children, *Fly By Night.* The book caused more controversy because he drew a naked boy. "I drew myself as a baby in it," he said. "You can see me in my mother's arms in the book's only double-spread picture."

Maurice Sendak illustrated the beloved Christmas story
The Nutcracker. For this effort he won the
New York Times Book Review Award.

HIS BEST WORK

By 1981, Sendak completed the third and last book in his trilogy, *Outside Over There.* Though *Where the Wild Things Are* received the most attention, Sendak considered *Outside Over There* his best work.

The book is related to his own childhood when his sister Natalie took care of him. His mother had to go out to work, so she handed him over to Natalie. Sendak spent a year on the pencil drawings, then showed them to friends. They urged him to publish drawings as they were and not paint them. At first, Sendak listened to them. But in the end, he knew the book had to be full color.

"I happen not to be interested in writing just for children," he said. *Outside Over There* can be read by children, it can be read by anybody. No other work of art has given me this inner peace and happiness. I have caught the thing that has eluded me for so long, so critical to living. And knowing that means everything, regardless of what anyone else says about the book."

A DREAM COME TRUE

Maurice Sendak has had a fulfilling and rewarding career as an illustrator. And he admits that he would not have it any other way.

"All my life I have been in the fortunate position of doing, creating, what came naturally to me," he said. "What could be more wonderful than a dream of childhood coming true? As a small boy, I pasted and clipped my bits of books together and hoped only for a life that would allow me to earn my bread by making books. And here I am all grown up, still staying home, pasting and clipping bits of books together."

In recent years, Sendak hasn't produced as many books as he has in the past. But he has established himself as a versatile and imaginative illustrator whose works will be cherished for decades to come.

GLOSSARY

Apprentice — any beginner; learner.

Backlist — a publisher's list of older titles kept in print.

Collaborate — two or more pople working together on the same project.

Confidante — a person to whom someone tells their secrets or private matters.

Crosshatch — to shade with two or more sets of intersecting parallel lines.

Editor — a person who reads through written material. An editor corrects the material so it is ready to be printed.

Illustrate — To provide a publication with pictures and diagrams.

Immune — not affected by disease or illness.

Mass produce — to manufacture goods in large quantities, using standard designs and assembly-line techniques.

Paperback — a book having a flexible paper binding.

Stammer — involuntary pause or break in speech.

Index